ALTERNATOR BOOKS™

THE REAL SCIENCE OF
INVISIBILITY

Christina Hill

Lerner Publications ◆ Minneapolis

Lerner Publications Company
An imprint of Lerner Publishing Group, Inc.
241 First Avenue North
Minneapolis, MN 55401 USA

For reading levels and more information, look up this title at www.lernerbooks.com.

Library of Congress Cataloging-in-Publication Data

Names: Hill, Christina, author.
Title: The real science of invisibility / by Christina Hill.
Description: Minneapolis : Lerner Publications, [2022] | Series: The real science of superpowers (alternator books) | Includes bibliographical references and index. | Audience: Ages 8–12 | Audience: Grades 4–6 | Summary: "It's easy for superpowered crimefighters to turn invisible and sneak up on bad guys. But what about real crimefighters? Find out how scientists are using technology to make things disappear before our eyes"— Provided by publisher.
Identifiers: LCCN 2021021684 (print) | LCCN 2021021685 (ebook) | ISBN 9781728441214 (library binding) | ISBN 9781728449579 (paperback) | ISBN 9781728445304 (ebook)
Subjects: LCSH: Invisibility—Juvenile literature. | Superheroes—Juvenile literature. | Information display systems—Juvenile literature. | Camouflage (Biology)—Juvenile literature.
Classification: LCC QC406 .H55 2021 (print) | LCC QC406 (ebook) | DDC 535—dc23

LC record available at https://lccn.loc.gov/2021021684
LC ebook record available at https://lccn.loc.gov/2021021685

Manufactured in the United States of America
1-49892-49735-7/7/2021

Getting ready in the morning would be a lot easier if you were invisible!

Beep, beep, beep. You groan as you reach over to turn off your alarm clock. It's time to get ready for school. Your hair is a mess, but you don't mind. You possess an invisibility cloak! With one swift motion, you drape the cloak over your head. Just like that, you disappear!

You head downstairs for breakfast and see your sister making cookies for a bake sale. You walk right past her, undetected. You snatch a cookie and take a huge bite. This is the best superpower ever!

Unfortunately, invisibility cloaks aren't real. But think about all the things you could do if they were! You could pull off the best magic tricks and win every game of hide-and-seek. You could work as a spy or secret agent. And you could help fight crime, just like a hero!

Magicians use tricks to make objects seem to disappear.

THE SCIENCE OF INVISIBILITY

We can see when light enters our eyes.

What does it mean to be invisible? First, let's look at how vision works. Humans can see objects that reflect light. When light hits an object, some of the light bounces off and goes to the eye. The light hits receptors in the eye that send messages to the brain. The brain interprets the messages into the color and shape of the object.

Without light, nothing is visible. This is why we can't see in the dark. A dark room may look empty, but it could be full of objects you can't see because there is no reflected light for your eyes to absorb.

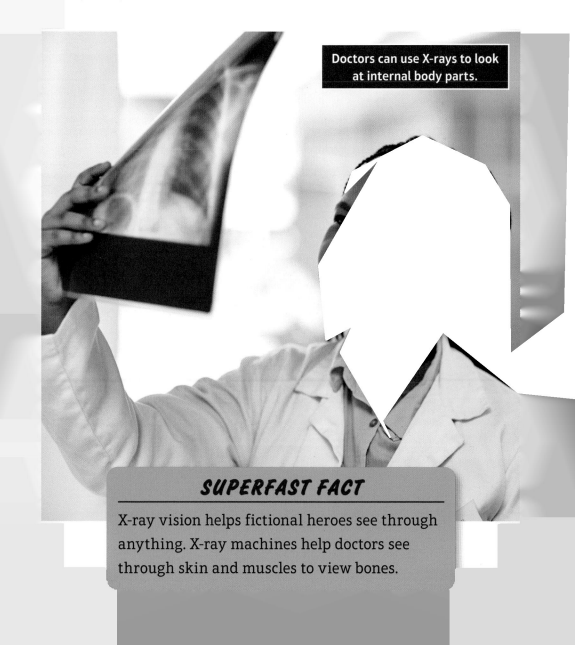

Doctors can use X-rays to look at internal body parts.

SUPERFAST FACT

X-ray vision helps fictional heroes see through anything. X-ray machines help doctors see through skin and muscles to view bones.

Our world is full of color. Each color has a different wavelength of light. The colors that we see are the wavelengths that are reflected and not absorbed by an object. A ripe banana looks yellow because it absorbs every color except yellow. The yellow wavelength reflects off the banana.

Bananas reflect yellow or green wavelengths of light depending on how ripe they are.

Wavelengths of light also bend at different angles. A prism is a triangular piece of glass. When light enters a prism, the wavelengths bend at different angles. The prism separates the light into individual colors that look like a rainbow.

Some light waves move around an object instead of bouncing off of it. If you look through a glass of water, the objects on the other side of the glass appear distorted. When light travels from air into water, the light changes direction and bends. This alters the way objects appear when we see them through water.

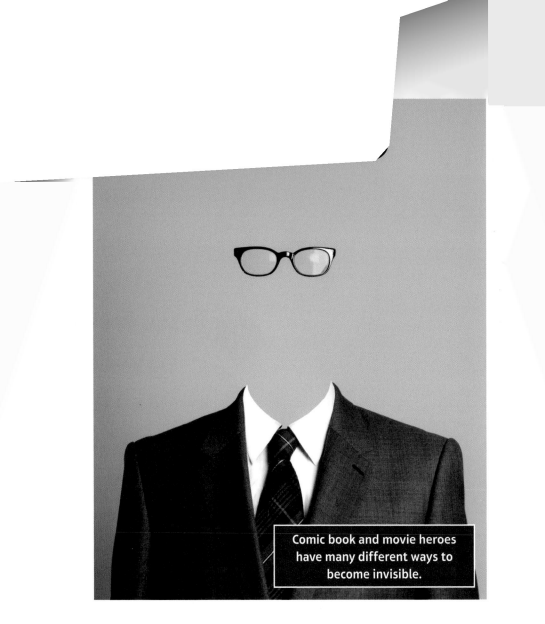

Comic book and movie heroes have many different ways to become invisible.

Fictional heroes can conceal themselves in different ways. Some heroes come from different planets and have special body parts that allow them to appear invisible. Others use magic or mind tricks to disappear. They might change colors to camouflage themselves, or even alter their body shape to hide behind objects.

A few heroes can alter their appearance to look exactly like someone else. Others fight crime at night, so they wear dark costumes and masks to blend into shadows and sneak up on villains unseen.

A motionless walking stick insect can blend in perfectly with plants.

SUPERFAST FACT

Walking stick insects look just like sticks! Their camouflage is a clever disguise that makes them invisible to predators.

Some animals are also masters of hiding in plain sight. Glass catfish, moon jellyfish, and glasswing butterflies have transparent body parts. Light passes through them instead of reflecting. They have see-through skin, muscles, or organs to help them appear invisible. Unfortunately, human bodies are not transparent!

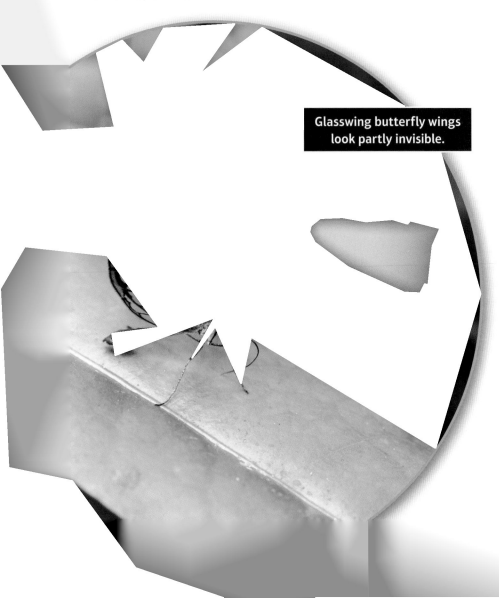

Glasswing butterfly wings look partly invisible.

Being transparent does not mean an object is invisible. Clear things are still visible. Think about glass, diamonds, or even water. We can see through them, but we still know they are there. Transparent heroes can appear invisible if someone isn't looking too closely. But you still might be able to see a wavy or distorted outline of their bodies as the light passes through them.

In order to be truly invisible, you need to completely block the reflection of light. But that is impossible. Or is it?

Water is transparent, but we can still see it in most situations.

CHAPTER 3
REAL-LIFE INVISIBILITY

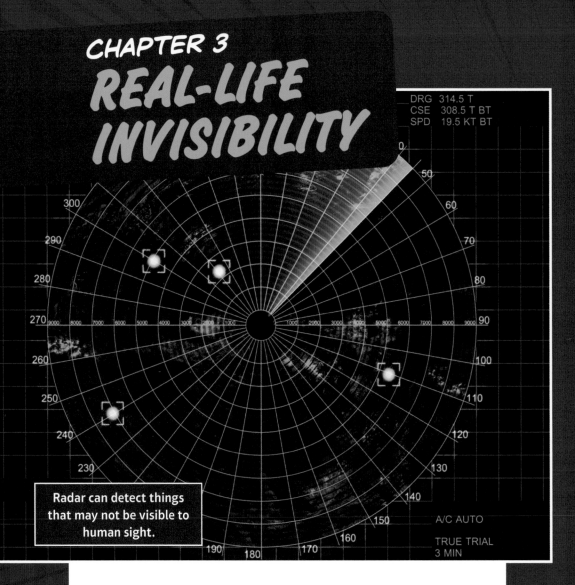

DRG 314.5 T
CSE 308.5 T BT
SPD 19.5 KT BT

A/C AUTO

TRUE TRIAL
3 MIN

Radar can detect things that may not be visible to human sight.

Some science fiction and fantasy heroes wear cloaks or capes made out of unique invisible materials to hide themselves. Others have special jewelry, like rings or crowns, with invisibility powers. They might have jets, motorcycles, or special suits that are invisible to radar. Radar systems use radio waves to find objects. The radio waves go out over large areas and then bounce back when they encounter objects.

Great horned owls blend into their surroundings.

AMAZING ANIMAL POWER

Owls aren't invisible or transparent, but they are hard to detect! Their feathers adapt to match their environment. Snowy owls are pure white like the snow. Great horned owls match the color of brown tree trunks. Owls can change their shape by standing tall and pulling in their feathers. This is similar to a child standing sideways behind a tree to stay hidden during a game of hide-and-seek.

B-2 stealth jets are invisible on radar.

Hiding stealth jets from radar is a real-life science superpower. Planes are usually curved, which makes them easy to detect. The rounded shapes help radar reflect and bounce back to the source of the radar. But stealth jets, like the B-2, are made of special flat shapes with sharp edges. When radio waves hit a stealth plane, they bounce off at an angle rather than going back to the radar source. This makes the aircraft invisible unless it is directly above the radar. Stealth jets are also sprayed with a coating that absorbs radar waves. They are often painted in dark colors that make them hard to see.

High-tech sensors in F-35 jets allow pilots to have a 360-degree view around them. With this technology, it is almost like the body of the jet itself isn't there. The pilots can see anyone or anything coming their way.

F-35 fighter jets are real-life stealth aircraft.

SUPERFAST FACT

Movie stunts are often filmed in front of a green screen. Using digital technology, technicians can then remove the green screen and replace it with any background.

Staying hidden is essential to real-life soldiers and spies on missions. Using the cover of darkness helps them stay stealthy and avoid reflecting light. But their bodies still give off infrared radiation. Infrared radiation is a wavelength of light that is not visible to humans, but we can feel it as heat. For example, body heat is infrared radiation that we can feel. But if a criminal is being sneaky, by the time you feel their body heat, it will be too late!

d light can tell us where
e are, even in the dark.

Infrared cameras can detect body heat, even in the dark. Even the darkest night will not be enough to help someone stay invisible. But in 2018, scientists created a bendable sheet made of silicon. It can hide up to ninety-four percent of infrared light! Carrying the sheet would allow soldiers to avoid detection by infrared cameras. Now that's real-life invisibility.

People use infrared cameras for many different reasons. Hospitals can use them to detect a person's body temperature.

Scientists have discovered another way to manipulate light. Ordinary materials like gold, metal, and fiberglass can be mixed together to form a metamaterial. The metamaterial can change the direction of light rays so that the light moves around it. Anything covered by the metamaterial is invisible! Metamaterials can also absorb sound waves.

Metamaterial samples can be made with a 3D printer.

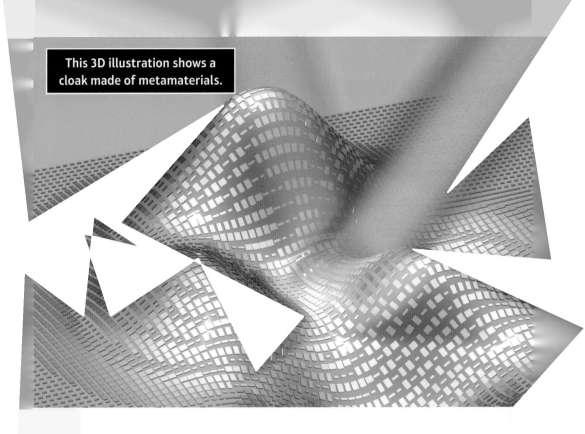

This 3D illustration shows a cloak made of metamaterials.

Could metamaterials be used to create a real-life invisibility cloak? A few challenges stand in the way. Metamaterials are tiny. They must be perfectly arranged on a microscopic level to bend the light waves from all directions. Scientists haven't been able to build enough to hide a human body.

Some metamaterials use detailed patterns to bend, or refract, light. The light bends around the metamaterial object, tricking us into thinking the object is not there. However, the pattern of the metamaterial has to line up perfectly to be effective. So when a person hiding underneath the material moves, they will be seen. And how would the wearer see? Adding eye holes would be a quick fix—but then their eyes would be visible!

THE FUTURE OF INVISIBILITY

Cutting-edge technology
could give us superpowers
in the future.

Scientists have many ideas about the power of invisibility. They have made progress in making science fiction a reality. Each improvement brings us one step closer to having superpowers.

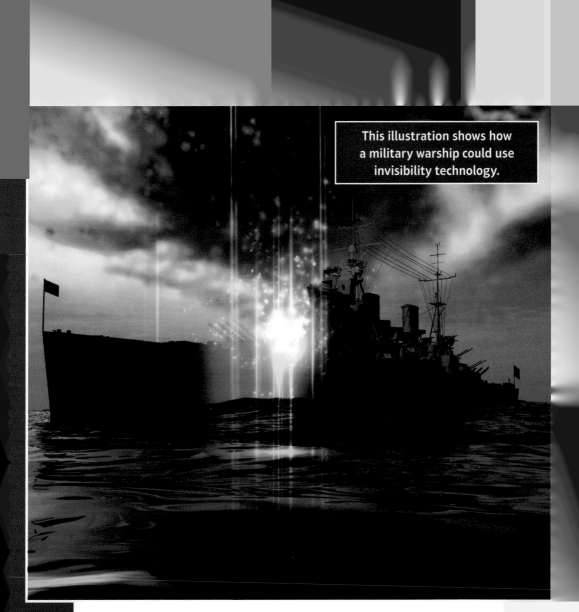

This illustration shows how a military warship could use invisibility technology.

Manipulating light with time cloaking is one way scientists could make invisibility a reality in the future. Light passes through a special lens, which splits the different wavelengths of light and creates a gap in the light's beam. Anything that happens during that gap is invisible. Then, scientists stitch the beam back together so quickly that the gap is not noticed.

Film directors make things disappear with camera tricks.

To understand how time cloaking works, think about how movies are made. Movie directors can make on-screen objects disappear by stopping the camera, moving them, and then starting the camera again. Even though you know the director moved the object, the actual movement wasn't visible to you because that portion of time was edited out. So, from your perspective, the object disappeared.

So far, scientists have only been able to create a gap in time that is less than a second. But this method opens up future options for humans to have hero-level invisibility.

These eggs could contain secret messages.

The science behind invisibility isn't just for sneaking up on friends or the ultimate game of hide-and-seek. It can be used to make a cloak of protection. Scientists are looking at using cloaking devices to protect buildings during earthquakes. The shockwave of the earthquake could pass around the building and keep the people inside safe. This same technology could hide buildings from tsunamis!

Earthquakes can cause a lot of damage.

Michael Selvanayagam (*left*) and George Eleftheriades (*right*) are researchers at the University of Toronto. They invented the first active invisibility cloak.

SUPER STEM BREAKTHROUGH

To solve some of the problems associated with wearing an invisibility cloak, scientists created a shield instead! In 2019, a company covered a glass shield with a light-bending material. The shield bends the light and makes objects hidden behind it invisible. It can hide a person, a plane, or even a building. It even hides objects from infrared waves. The shield is intended for military use as a way to keep soldiers safe.

While many fictional heroes have the power of invisibility, sometimes villains do too. There is a lot of responsibility that comes with being invisible. It would be easy for criminals to commit crimes if nobody could see them. Scientists and government officials need to make sure this superpower is used for good and not evil. At its best, invisibility technology will help humans get a little closer to the realm of superbeings.

Even if you can't make yourself invisible, you can send hidden messages to a friend! All you need is an acid-based liquid such as milk, lemon juice, or vinegar. Dip a cotton swab or toothpick into the liquid and write your message on a blank piece of paper. Deliver the message to a friend. Tell them to have an adult help to heat the paper with a hairdryer, hot iron, or by holding the paper over a warm light bulb. The acid will turn brown, allowing your invisible message to appear!

camouflage: the hiding or disguising of something by covering it up or changing the way it looks

infrared: a wavelength of light that is outside the visual spectrum

light wave: a wave of moving energy that makes up light

metamaterial: an artificial material made by combining other materials

radar: a device that sends out radio waves to locate the position and speed of a moving object such as an airplane

receptor: a nerve ending that senses changes in light, temperature, and pressure

reflect: to bend or throw back waves of light, sound, or heat

refract: to make light change direction when it passes from one medium to another

stealth: an aircraft designed to produce a very weak radar return

transparent: clear enough or thin enough to be seen through

Colón, Erica I. *Awesome Physics Experiments for Kids: 40 Fun Science Projects and Why They Work.* Emeryville, CA: Rockridge Press, 2019.

Hoena, Blake. *Invisibility.* Minneapolis: Bellwether Media, 2021.

If Superpowers Were Real: Invisibility
https://ed.ted.com/lessons/if-superpowers-were-real-invisibility-joy-lin

Kuromiya, Jun. *The Future of Entertainment.* Minneapolis: Lerner Publications, 2021.

Optics 4 Kids
https://www.optics4kids.org

Prism (Optics) Facts for Kids
https://kids.kiddle.co/Prism_(optics)

Refraction Facts for Kids
https://kids.kiddle.co/Refraction

Scirri, Kaitlin. *The Science of Invisibility and X-ray Vision.* New York: Cavendish Square, 2019.

Index

Photo Acknowledgments

Image credits: sturti/Getty Images, p.4; Sean Gladwell/Getty Images, p.5; Carmelo Geraci/EyeEm/Getty Images, p.6; PeopleImages/Getty Images, p.7; fitri iskandar zakariah/Getty Images, p.8; Nicholas Rigg/Getty Images, p.9; Thomas Jackson/ Getty Images, p.10; natfu/Getty Images, p.11; Helaine Weide/Getty Images, p.12; Ascent/PKS Media Inc./Getty Images, p.13; enot-poloskun/Getty Images, p.14; Paul Bruch Photography/Getty Images, p.15; danku/Getty Images, p.16; ChrisAyre/ Getty Images, p.17; Cultura RM Exclusive/Joseph Giacomin/Getty Images, p.18; PongMoji/Getty Images, p.19; WLADIMIR BULGAR/SCIENCE PHOTO LIBRARY/ Getty Images, p.20; Xinhua/Xinhua News Agency/Newscom, p.21; Holloway/Getty Images, p.22; VICTOR HABBICK VISIONS/SCIENCE PHOTO LIBRARY/Newscom, p.23; philipimage/Getty Images, p.24; La Bicicleta Vermella/Getty Images, p.25; Mirga Gnter/EyeEm/Getty Images, p.26; Richard Lautens/ZUMA Press/Newscom, p.27; Witthaya Prasongsin/Getty Images, p.28; Alexander Gold/Shutterstock, p.29;

Cover: Ollyy/Shutterstock